Annabelle

Sandra Grace

Sandra Fram

Sandra Fram

Copyright © 2022, 2025 by Sandra Grace
All rights reserved

No part of this publication may be reproduced, distributed, or transmitted in any form or by any means, including photocopying, recording, or other electronic or mechanical methods, without the prior written permission of the author, except as permitted by Canadian copyright law. For permission requests, contact Sandra Grace at sgracewrites@outlook.com.

"As for God, His way is perfect..." Psalm 18:30.

Scripture from the King James Version, public domain;
The New American Standard Bible®, copyright © 1960, 1962, 1963, 1968, 1971, 1972, 1973, 1975, 1977, 1995 by The Lockman Foundation. Used by permission;
And the Holy Bible, English Standard Version, copyright © 2001 by Crossway Bibles, a publishing ministry of Good News Publishers. Used by permission. All rights reserved.

Annabelle photos by Andrea Parks (Now I Lay Me Down to Sleep). Used by permission.

Second Edition 2025

Contents

VII	Dedication
01	Annabelle
08	Annabelle's Story
11	From Annabelle's Nauna
12	Remember
13	Scripture
14	From Annabelle's Grandma
15	Grief
16	Scripture
17	From Annabelle's Mother
19	Notes
22	Excerpts from Revelation 21 & 22
24	Resources and Contacts

As for God, His way is perfect

Annabelle Hope Ironside
April 29, 2019

Gift of God

STOCK PHOTO

Annabelle

My entrance into the world brought a rush of sensations—of haste, of cold and bright light and noise, of pain and fear. Of comfort in your soft voices and love in your arms.

I remember you—your touch, so gentle. You held me. You stroked my cheek. You kissed me. I felt your heartbeat that I knew so well...the rise and fall of your chest as you drew me close. You sang to me, a melody I carry with me even now.

You called me Annabelle. Annabelle Hope.

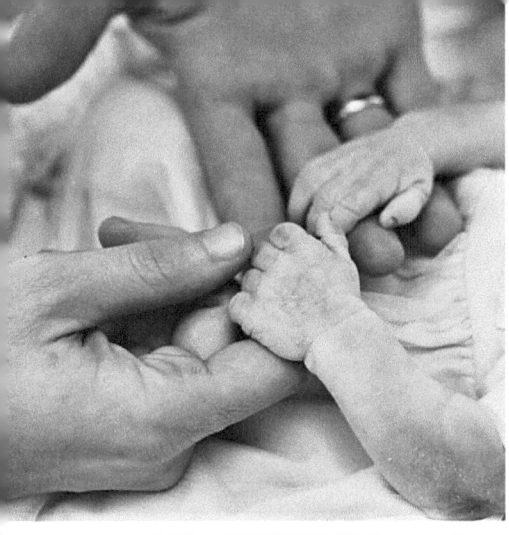

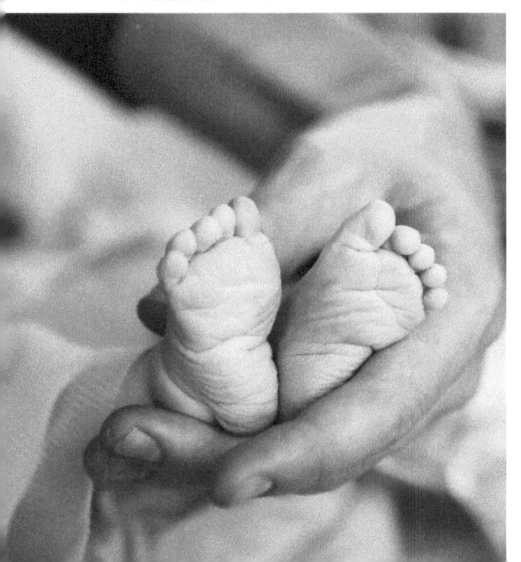

I wanted to stay with you; you were so safe and so good. I belonged right there with you. I thought I was yours and you were mine for a lifetime. I snuggled in...

But it wasn't to be. You both knew I could not stay. You had prepared for my coming and my going all at once. I couldn't understand it then. I didn't know what was happening. You looked on me with trails of wet on your faces. Why did you cry for me? Sweet Mother... Dear Daddy...

If you could have seen what was coming... If you could have known...

You treasured me for the few minutes I was with you, then you let me go. I felt a tiny shudder pass through you...heard the catch in your throats as you gave me back to my Father.

My every breath,
long and clear and deep,
was suddenly filled with
the fragrance of Heaven

He called my name, and I knew release from all those earthly restrictions. I felt no more the weight of that life. In an instant, I was changed. The pain and the fear were gone and so were you.

No longer an infant... No longer confined to frailty and sin of the flesh, I was free and pure. I was granted knowledge and wisdom and understanding beyond anything any mortal can know. My every breath, long and clear and deep, was suddenly filled with the fragrance of Heaven. How good it felt!

And *He* was there.

I saw my Savior's smile, and nothing else mattered. Oh, the joy that flooded through me! His brilliant light and warmth surrounded me. His holiness and love and justice were all I saw. Every other thought and memory fled away. There was only joy in my Lord, marvel at His glory, wonder at the beauty of His Heaven, and awe at the immensity of His pardon. Yes, my pardon from sin.

I fell at His feet in humility, in gratitude and reverence. He reached for me. "Well done, my daughter," He told me. "Glory is brought to my name because of the life of Annabelle."

STOCK PHOTO

It was all in a flash, everything at once, and it continues even yet. Each moment is an extension of the one before. Everything rushes and everything stands still. Time, which so constrains those on earth, has no place here. The sun never sets, the sky never darkens, and the day is never cold.

My Father's house—endless...magnificent. Its arches glisten with a radiance that never dims. Jasper; emeralds; sapphires; translucent gold... Brilliant colors of His rainbow stretch across my Father's throne. My Redeemer is its King, the morning star, the holy temple. He speaks with thunder, and lightning flashes from sky to sky. His glory and majesty fill its heights and reach to its farthest corners. No words exist in human tongue to tell such wonders.

It's all still new to me. I see it again and again for the first time, and I marvel anew with greater awe than before. Every joy I know—every adoration and praise—erupts to the fullest from within me, and I can't hold back uttermost worship of the Lamb. To Him be power, honor, riches, and blessing for evermore!

Through gates of pearl, across long pink skies, I watch and listen. Do you know that I think about you? I do. I'm drawn to you. I know you. I know I'm yours. One day you will join me here, and I'll welcome you to our home. Oh, wait till you see!

Sometimes, you miss me, but I don't know what that is. I've never missed anything; my Father's house lacks nothing.

We will praise Him because He gave me to you and because He took me away; His ways are perfect

---

There's a glint in your eye when you think of me, but I can't understand it. I've never been sad. I've not experienced loss. I don't ache for you the way you ache for me. I can only ponder such a mystery.

You speak of me, remembering our moments together. You wonder what I would look like now if I had stayed—my hair, my eyes, my smile. And it pleases me even more to know that I am loved by you still.

Miss me, yes, sweet family. But don't wish me back. I don't want to experience sin. I don't want to taint the name of Jesus or bring dishonor to my God.

Come to me soon, sweet Mother and Daddy, and bring my brothers with you. I hope for that day, not with longing but with expectation, when we will enjoy our God together. We will praise Him because He gave me to you and because He took me away; His ways are perfect. We will walk side-by-side with our Savior in light and harmony, music and laughter, delight and perfection, and endless adoration of our Lord. What a day it will be, when we are together again!

Until then, my family, I cannot wait for you—what is waiting? There is so much of Paradise yet to discover. I am swept up and away in the glories of Heaven, without flaw and without stain. Tides of worship overflow me. The songs of the redeemed pour from my lips. I dance to melodies more beautiful than angels' song, for I cannot contain my utter joy.

So wait for me, dear Daddy and Mother, until you fulfill your time on earth.

Wait for me.
Think of me.
Smile for me.

And I am here until you come.

by Sandra Grace

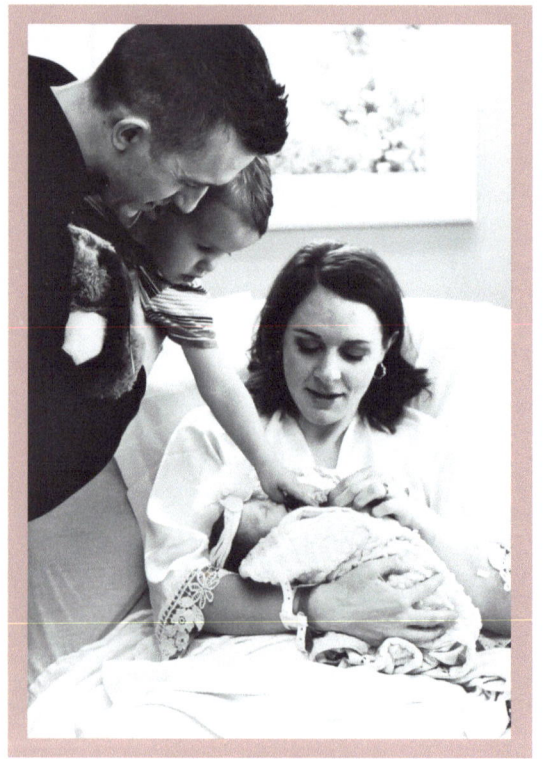

Annabelle's Story

Eighteen weeks into pregnancy, a routine ultrasound revealed that baby Annabelle was missing one kidney and the other kidney was not developing properly, rendering it non-functional. A further complication of this condition was the under-development of her tiny lungs.

The prognosis was heartbreaking: inside the womb, little Annabelle was active and growing...safe, but she would not be able to survive more than a few minutes—maybe hours—after birth.

Amidst the questions and grief that enveloped her parents over the next few months, one constant prevailed: their little girl belonged to God, her life was in His hands, and He makes no mistakes.

Their prayer was for a miracle, knowing that God could reverse her condition and save Annabelle's life...that she could be born healthy and whole.

But this was not to be.

Annabelle's Story
Continued

Yet they refused to let their grief turn their hearts cold. They would cling to their God. They would praise and thank Him for the tiny life He'd given them, however long. Whatever His plan and purpose for their little one, "It is well with my soul" was their cry.

Annabelle Hope came into the world seven weeks early on April 29, 2019. She lived for 40 minutes and then went to be with her Heavenly Father.

Even in their tears, Annabelle's parents still praise God, for they hold fast to the promise that they will see her again. They know where their daughter is and that she is more alive now than ever possible here on earth. She is whole, free of pain, dancing in the glories of Heaven—the only life Annabelle has ever known.

*For You [God] formed my inward parts;
You knitted me together
in my mother's womb.
...I am fearfully and wonderfully made.
Wonderful are Your works...*

Psalm 139:13 & 14

Dear Grieving Friend,

    The mother's pain of loss is something I know well, for I have been there too. And I am there again after the loss of my newborn granddaughter.

    As time goes by, we fear others will forget and will tell us "it is time to move on" (if we dare to share our hearts).

    Please know, I am crying with you while praying God's comfort and grace for you each day. We are promised these tears will be wiped away forever and separation will be no longer.

    May your heart be drawn to learn the preciousness of Christ as you journey life with this love and loss.

Blessings to you each day,
Annabelle's "Nauna," Bethany Ironside

Remember

Over and over come the words from well-meaning family and friends—

"You need to get over it..."

"Time to move on..."

And the grieving parents are broken-hearted yet again that they must stuff their pain and their memories back inside, so others won't have to see them.

There will come a time, dear Mother and Father, when your tears will no longer be right at the edge...when your grief won't be just at the surface, ready to spill out. Someday, you will be able to set this aside for a little while and think of other things.

But no parent or grandparent can ever get over the loss of a child. There's no need to conform to that expectation. No need to hide away all signs of the precious life that filled your hopes and dreams, the one who still lives on in your hearts.

Wrap around you whatever memories you have of your little one. Speak his name. Keep her pictures on the mantle. He is your son. She is your daughter. Forever missed. Forever loved.

Take comfort that your baby is safe in the arms of the Savior, free of all sickness and pain, more alive now than ever before, forever joyful in the glories and perfection of Heaven.

Scripture

Weeping may endure for a night,
but joy cometh in the morning.
Psalm 30:5

Be merciful to me, Lord, for I am in distress;
my eyes grow weak with sorrow,
my soul and body with grief.
Psalm 31:9

The Lord is near
to them that are brokenhearted;
and saves those who are crushed in spirit.
Psalm 34:18

Why, my soul, are you downcast?
Why so disturbed within me?
Put your hope in God,
for I will yet praise Him, my Savior and my God.
Psalm 42:11

Trust in Him at all times; ye people,
pour out your heart before Him:
God is a refuge to us.
Psalm 62:8

My flesh and my heart may fail,
but God is the strength of my heart
and my portion forever.
Psalm 73:26

Dear Grandma,

Losing our precious Annabelle was profoundly painful. A grandchild is not supposed to pass before the grandparent. All the hopes, dreams, and future memories with her disappeared. In addition to this unbearable loss was a second layer of grief: that helpless feeling as I stood by and watched my daughter and son-in-law in tears, grieving the loss of their baby.

A grandmother's grief is unique; and unless they have been on this journey, very few understand. Grandmothers' grief is double-layered: we are not only grieving the loss of our precious grandchildren, but we are also heartbroken and grieving for our suffering daughters and sons. We are mothers. We hurt when our children hurt. We want to comfort them, but we can't change the situation or bring the babies back.

The grief journey is heart-rending, and at times you may feel alone. But our God of Hope and Comfort walks with you.

It may take time, but talk about your grandchild to others. Say his or her name. Let your daughter and son know that you miss their little one. Acknowledge your grandbaby in conversation. Include him when you're asked the number of your grandchildren. Celebrate her birthday.

Never forget that this life was of value, this child mattered and left a mark. Psalm 139:13-14.

Annabelle's Grandma, Nancy Whitworth

Grief

The loss of a child is the most devastating thing a parent can endure. It cuts deep into the soul. Grief can take over every part of life until you can't feel anything else, you can't breathe, and you can't even see the sky. There seems to be no way out.

Allowing your grief is a necessary part of the healing process. It's okay to feel it. It's even okay, for a while, to be pulled under by its fierce tides. Your loss is heavy, and your world is breaking apart right now. There's no need to rush to put all the pieces back together just yet.

Run to God with your pain and empty out your heart to Him. *"In my distress…I cried to my God for help. He heard my voice …"* Psalm 18:6 (NASB)

Go to someone you trust, one who will listen and will let you pour out everything in you. Say it—whatever's on your heart—as many times as you need to. Speaking it aloud is a vital step to healing.

Grieve the child that was taken too soon. Grieve the little one you never got to meet. Give your baby a name, even if it was too young for you to know if it was a boy or a girl. Talk about her. Give him a place in your family.

In its time, a measure of healing will come, and grief will step back into the shadows. Yes, you will carry this child forever in your heart; you wouldn't want it any other way.

But one day, you will learn to laugh again.

Scripture

*My help comes from the Lord,
the Maker of Heaven and earth.*
Psalm 121:2

[Lord,] May your unfailing love be my comfort.
Psalm 119:76

*He heals the brokenhearted
and binds up their wounds.*
Psalm 147:3

*But those who hope in the Lord
will renew their strength.
They will soar on wings like eagles;
they will run and not grow weary,
they will walk and not be faint.*
Isaiah 40:31

*May the God of hope fill you
with all joy and peace as you trust in Him,
so you may overflow with hope.*
Romans 15:13

*Blessed be God, even the Father
of our Lord Jesus Christ,
the Father of mercies
and the God of all comfort.*
2 Corinthians 1:3

Dear Mama,

   You read this with a broken heart over the loss of your precious baby. Your child is a beautiful and unique gift from God, worthy of all the love, grief, and remembrance you pour over it. I am so sorry for your loss. I know the deep ache of empty arms.

   In this season of tears, take care of your soul. As the Lord holds your baby tightly in His hands right now, may you cling just as tightly to the promises of Scripture. While we await the day when we will be reunited, first with Christ, and then with our dear children, be still. Right now, Mama, "Be still and know that I am God." (Psalm. 46:10)

   Lean into Jesus. In every way, in every moment. When you feel it's all you can do. Run to Him and make Him your lifeline. Immerse yourself fully in Scripture. Rely on concrete truth, rather than the ever-changing emotions of each day. Mama, with your soul, be still.

   Live in this season. Fully. Embrace it. It is a season of grief. Let yourself grieve. Slow down. Take those extra events off the calendar. Cry and mourn. Smile and laugh. Just don't block out the grief. Mama, with your life, be still.

    Keep your eyes wide open. Neither close your eyes to the world around you nor dart about so busily that you don't see what is in front of you. Let your eyes rest on the generosity, kindness, and encouragement shown to you by others. While your heart is heavy, there are prayers being answered all around you. Don't neglect to see them. These are the pillars that will strengthen your faith in the years to come. They are a testament to the faithfulness of your God so you can proclaim His goodness. See it, take it in, write it down, and store it up in your heart. Mama, with your eyes, be still.

    As the days begin to pass, embrace them. With the memory of your baby adorning your thoughts, begin to live life once again. This is possible through the freedom and hope you have in Christ. You need not move forward in fear because you will never forget the sweet child you were given. You will never forget the life. You will never forget the love. You, Mama, will never forget.

    And one day, all things will be redeemed.

    But today, Mama, be still and know.

Sincerely,
Annabelle's Mommy, Kristen Ironside

Thoughts

Prayer

Revelation 21 & 22

*And God shall wipe away all tears from their eyes;
and there shall be no more death, neither sorrow nor
crying, neither shall there be any more pain:
for the former things are passed away.*

*...And the city was pure gold, like unto clear glass.
And the foundations of the wall were garnished
with precious stones...jasper...sapphire...emerald...
beryl...topaz...amethyst...*

*Each one of the gates was a single pearl.
And the street of the city was pure gold,
as it were transparent glass.*

*And the city had no need of the sun...
for the glory of God did lighten it...
for there shall be no night there...*

*And there shall be no more curse;
but the throne of God and of the Lamb shall be in it;
and His servants shall serve Him:
and they shall see His face;
and His name shall be in their foreheads...
and they shall reign forever and ever...*

*"Behold, I come quickly...
I am Alpha and Omega, the beginning and the end,
the first and the last...the bright and morning star..."*

Amen. Even so, come, Lord Jesus.

Excerpts from the KJV

This story of Annabelle, her photographs, and these letters are made available with the permission of the Ironside family

For more on Annabelle Hope or to connect with Kristen Ironside, Annabelle's mother, go online to

    Fearfully and Wonderfully Made: The Life, Loss, and Lessons of Annabelle Hope

To connect with the author
    Email: sgracewrites@outlook.com
    Visit her website: wingsinthestorm.ca

Further resource
    Safe in the Arms of God, by John MacArthur

Romans 3:23 & 6:23. "All have sinned and come short of the glory of God. For the wages of sin is death, but the gift of God is eternal life through Jesus Christ our Lord." (KJV)

John 14:6. "Jesus said...I am the way and the truth and the life; no one comes to the Father except through me.

I John 1:9. "If we confess our sins, He is faithful and just to forgive us our sins and to cleanse us from all unrighteousness." (KJV)

Acts 3:19. "Repent...that your sins may be blotted out." (ESV)

Ephesians 2:8 & 9. "For by grace you have been saved through faith; and this is not of yourselves, it is the gift of God; not a result of works, so that no one may boast." (NASB)

Philippians 3:20 & 21. "Our citizenship is in Heaven...[Jesus Christ] will transform our lowly body to be like His glorious body..." (ESV)